Your Skin and Mine

This Is a Let's-Read-and-Find-Out Science Book®

REVISED EDITION

Your Skin and Mine

by Paul Showers • illustrated by Kathleen Kuchera

HarperCollins*Publishers*

The *Let's-Read-and-Find-Out Science* book series was originated by Dr. Franklyn M. Branley, Astronomer Emeritus and former Chairman of the American Museum–Hayden Planetarium, and was formerly co-edited by him and Dr. Roma Gans, Professor Emeritus of Childhood Education, Teachers College, Columbia University. Text and illustrations for each of the books in the series are checked for accuracy by an expert in the relevant field. For more information about Let's-Read-and-Find-Out Science books, write to HarperCollins Children's Books, 195 Broadway, New York, NY 10007.

Your Skin and Mine
Text copyright © 1965, 1991 by Paul Showers
Illustrations copyright © 1991 by Kathleen Kuchera
All rights reserved. No part of this book may be
used or reproduced in any manner whatsoever without
written permission except in the case of brief quotations
embodied in critical articles and reviews.
Manufactured in China.
For information address HarperCollins Children's Books,
a division of HarperCollins Publishers,
195 Broadway, New York, NY 10007.
21 SCP 20 19 18
Revised Edition

Library of Congress Cataloging-in-Publication Data
Showers, Paul.
  Your skin and mine / by Paul Showers ; illustrated by Kathleen
Kuchera. — Rev. ed.
      p.   cm. — (Let's-read-and-find-out science. Stage 2)
  Summary: Explains the basic properties of skin, how it protects
the body, and how it can vary in color.
  ISBN 0-06-022522-X.—ISBN 0-06-022523-8 (lib. bdg.)
  ISBN 0-06-445102-X (pbk.)
  1. Skin—Juvenile literature. [1. Skin.] I. Kuchera, Kathleen,
ill. II. Title. III. Series.
QP88.5.S47   1991   90-37430
612.7′9—dc20   CIP
                                                           AC

The illustrations for YOUR SKIN AND MINE were prepared
on D'Arches cover stock with watercolor, pencil, and ink.

Mary's skin is light brown. So is Henry's. Mark's skin is dark brown. My skin is white with freckles.

Mary and Henry and Mark are in my class at school.

The other day our teacher passed out some magnifying glasses. Mary and Mark and Henry and I took turns looking at our skin under a magnifying glass. You can do the same thing.

Hair is part of your skin. With a magnifying glass you can look at the hair that grows out of your skin. Short hairs grow on your arms and legs. Long hairs grow on your head. Each hair grows out of a little hole called a follicle.

A follicle is a kind of tiny pocket. The hair grows up from the bottom of the follicle. It sticks out of the follicle the way a flower sticks out of a vase. A follicle has oil in it. The oil keeps the hair soft and shiny. It oozes out of the follicle and helps keep the skin from getting too dry.

Look at your fingertips under the magnifying glass. You can see loops and lines. They are ridges in your skin. You can make prints of the ridges on your fingertips.

Rub your fingers in some fingerpaint. Press the tips down on a piece of white paper. Lift your hand carefully. Your fingerprints show loops and lines. You can see them better under a magnifying glass.

This is one of Mary's fingerprints under the magnifying glass.

This is Mark's fingerprint.

This is Henry's.

Everybody's fingerprints are different.

Fingernails and toenails are part of your skin. They protect the tips of your fingers and toes. They are like your hair, because they keep growing all the time.

When you cut your hair, you don't feel anything. When you cut your nails, you don't feel anything either.

The rest of your skin has feeling. You can test this with a little
game. It goes like this.

One of us is blindfolded. Then the rest of us try to touch him
so gently he can't feel it.

We touch him gently on his cheek—his wrist—his leg. We
touch him with a paintbrush—and a feather. It is hard to fool
him. He can feel even a very light touch on his skin.

Your skin helps you to keep cool. On a hot day you become sweaty. Sweat is water that comes from inside your body. Your skin lets it out through tiny holes called pores. As the sweat dries, your skin becomes cooler.

Most of the pores in your skin are smaller than hair follicles. You cannot see the pores, even with a magnifying glass. But you can see the drops of sweat that come out of them.

EPIDERMIS

DERMIS

Your skin has two layers. The inside layer is called the dermis. There is blood in the dermis. The outside layer is called the epidermis. There is no blood in the epidermis.

The epidermis keeps rubbing off a little bit at a time. When you rub yourself hard with a towel, you often rub off a bit of your epidermis. It comes off in little pieces, all rolled up. When these little pieces of epidermis flake off, there is always more epidermis underneath.

Sometimes you rub off more epidermis than you want to. The other day we were climbing trees. I slid down too fast and skinned my leg. I scraped off a piece of epidermis. Part of it was wrinkled up at one side of the scraped place.

19

I could see the dermis layer of my skin. It was pink. It stung and smarted, but it didn't bleed. A clear, sticky fluid oozed out of the dermis until it covered all of the scraped part. That made the dermis stop smarting, and we went on playing.

In a half hour, the sticky fluid had dried and made a crust, which is called a scab. My father says a scab is like a bandage. It keeps germs out until new epidermis can grow. Then the scab falls off.

Yesterday Mary cut her finger when she opened a can of pet food for her cat. The cut went through the epidermis and into the dermis. Blood came out of the cut.

Her mother washed Mary's hand with soap and water. Then she put a bandage over the cut. That was to help stop the bleeding and to keep germs out.

Your body is all wrapped up in skin. It covers your body from the top of your head to the soles of your feet. Your skin helps to keep germs and dirt out of your body.

Skin also protects the body from the sun. It does this by making grains of color called melanin. Melanin grains are brown. They are very tiny. They are so tiny you can't even see one of them under a magnifying glass. There are millions of melanin grains in the skin. They are like a screen. They protect the body from the burning rays of sunlight.

Everybody's skin makes melanin. Some skin makes a lot of melanin. Other skin doesn't make very much. Mark's skin makes a lot of melanin. Henry's skin and Mary's skin do not make as much melanin as Mark's.

25

When the sun is very bright, the skin makes more melanin to screen out the burning light. That is why your skin gets darker when you play outside in the summer.

My skin makes very little melanin. Some of it is gathered in spots. These are my freckles. In summer my skin does not make enough melanin to screen out the sun's burning rays. I have to rub a sunscreen lotion on my skin. If I don't, I can get a painful sunburn.

Mary, Henry, and Mark will also get sunburns if they don't wear a sunscreen. Their skin won't burn as fast as mine, but the sun can burn even very dark skin.

Skin is easy to keep clean. It is easier to clean than cloth or almost anything. Yesterday my sister and I helped Mother clean up the attic. Mother made us wear our bathing suits. The attic was full of dust and cobwebs. We got sweaty and very dirty.

When we finished, we soaped ourselves and turned the hose
on each other. In two minutes we were clean again. Mother said
it was easier than washing our dirty clothes.

Mother made us cold lemonade. We sat on the steps. The breeze blew on our wet skin. We were cool, inside and out.